SENSES

SIGHT

Anita Ganeri

W
FRANKLIN WATTS
LONDON • SYDNEY

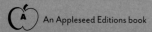 An Appleseed Editions book

Paperback edition 2017
First published in 2015 by Franklin Watts

© 2012 Appleseed Editions

Created by Appleseed Editions Ltd,
Well House, Friars Hill, Guestling,
East Sussex TN35 4ET

Designed and illustrated by Guy Callaby
Edited by Mary-Jane Wilkins

A CIP record for this book is available from the British Library

ISBN 978-1-4451-3254-9

Dewey Classification: 612.8'4

Picture acknowledgements
l = left, r = right, c = centre, t = top, b = bottom
page 1 forestpath/Shutterstock; 2 Cherry-Merry/Shutterstock;
3t iStockphoto/Thinkstock, c jeka84/Shutterstock, b Ron
Chapple Studios/Thinkstock; 4 AISPIX by Image Source/
Shutterstock; 6 Evgeny Tyzhinov/Shutterstock; 7 Karl
Weatherly/Thinkstock; 8 Nick Daly/Thinkstock; 9t Hemera/
Thinkstock, b iStockphoto/Thinkstock; 10 iStockphoto/
Thinkstock; 11 aleks.k/Shutterstock; 13 Polka Dot/Thinkstock;
14 Shutterstock; 15 Hemera/Thinkstock; 16l zhangyang/
Shutterstock, r Alekcey/Shutterstock; 17 vadim kozlovsky/
Shutterstock; 18 Digital Vision/Thinkstock; 19 Christopher
Robbins/Thinkstock; 20 CHEN WEI SENG/Shutterstock;
21 Boris Djuranovic/Shutterstock; 22 Ingram Publishing/
Thinkstock; 23 iStockphoto/Thinkstock; image beneath folios
iStockphoto/Thinkstock
Cover: iStockphoto/Thinkstock

Printed in China

MIX
Paper from
responsible sources
FSC® C104740

FSC
www.fsc.org

Franklin Watts
An imprint of Hachette Children's Group
Part of The Watts Publishing Group
Carmelite House
50 Victoria Embankment
London EC4Y 0DZ

An Hachette UK Company
www.hachette.co.uk

www.franklinwatts.co.uk

Contents

Eye spy 4

What can you see? 6

How do you see? 8

Inside your eyes 10

Sight messages 12

Two eyes 14

Seeing colours 16

Wearing glasses 18

Being blind 20

Sight facts 22

Useful words 24

Index 24

Eye spy

What happens when you look at a picture? What can you see?

What are you drawing?
What does your picture look like?

Sight is one of your senses. Your senses tell you about the world around you.

Your five senses are:

sight

hearing

touch

taste

smell

You see with your eyes

You hear with your ears

You touch with your fingers

You taste with your tongue

You smell with your nose

What can you see?

You can see lots of different **shapes** and **colours**.
Look at these blocks.

You can see things that are far away.

You can see things that are close up.

How do you see?

You see things with your two eyes. Light bounces off objects and goes into your eyes.

pupil

The light goes through two little black holes in the middle of your eyes. They are called pupils.

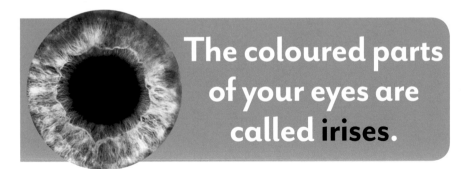

The coloured parts of your eyes are called **irises**.

Inside your eyes

There are tiny lenses inside your eyes. They shine the light on to the back of your eyes.

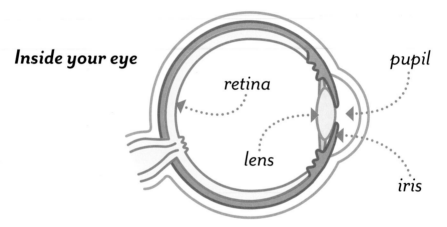

Inside your eye

retina

pupil

lens

iris

Your eyeballs are made from jelly that keeps your eyes in shape.

The lenses bend the light so that it makes a picture of what you are looking at.

Your eyes make a picture of dandelion flowers.

Sight messages

The picture on the back of your eye is upside down. **Nerves** send it to your brain.

What your eye sees

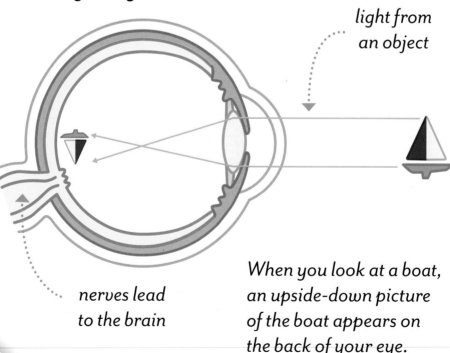

light from an object

nerves lead to the brain

When you look at a boat, an upside-down picture of the boat appears on the back of your eye.

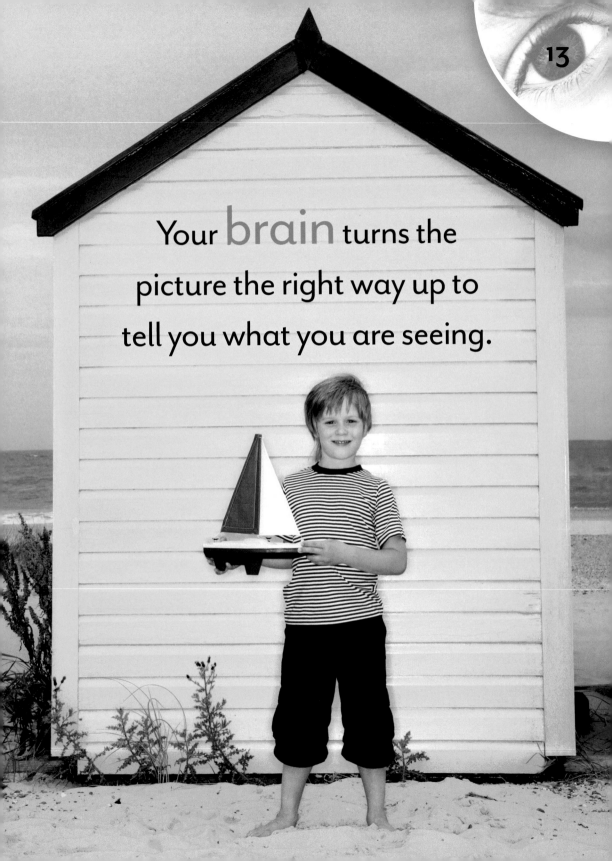

Your **brain** turns the picture the right way up to tell you what you are seeing.

Two eyes

Close one eye,
then the other.
What can you see?
Now open both
eyes. This gives
you a better view
of things.

When you are playing a sport, you need to be able to see all around you.

Your two eyes are on your head at the top of your body so that you can look all around.

Seeing colours

Some people can't see **colours** properly. They find it hard to tell red and green apart.

Can you see the difference between red and green objects?

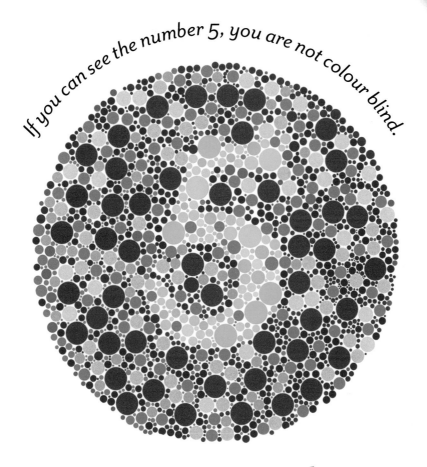

If you can see the number 5, you are not colour blind.

This is called being colour blind. It happens because some nerves in their eyes don't work very well.

Wearing glasses

Do you wear glasses to help you see things that are close up or far away?

Glasses are like extra lenses. They help your eyes to see clearly. Otherwise, everything looks fuzzy.

Being blind

Some people can't see at all, or can only see very little. This is called being blind.

In this race, a blind runner has another runner to help him find the way.

Guide dogs are trained to help blind people outside and in their homes.

Some blind people have a specially trained dog to help them find their way around.

Sight facts

Your eyelashes stop dust and dirt from getting into your eyes.

The muscles in your eyelids make you blink about 20,000 times a day. Blinking coats your eyes with tears that wash away germs and dirt.

A giant squid has eyes about twice the size of footballs. This makes them the biggest eyes of any animal.

Jumping spiders don't just have two eyes. They have eight eyes, arranged in three rows.

Useful words

irises
The coloured parts of your eyes. They can be blue, green, grey or brown.

nerves
Long, thin wires inside your body that send messages between your brain and body.

lenses
Clear discs inside your eyes that focus light so you can see clearly.

pupils
Little holes in the middle of your eyes that light passes through.

Index

being blind 20
being color blind 16, 17
brain 12, 13

eyeballs 10

five senses 5

glasses 18, 19
guide dogs 21

irises 9

lenses 10, 11, 19
light 8, 9

nerves 12, 17

pupils 9

two eyes 14, 15